GRANNY LOVES YOU

Armita Zadeh

To all the Grannies, the world's greatest expert on hugs, with love and giggles as sweet as her secret cookie recipe.

All rights reserved by Armita Zadeh. No part of this publication may be reproduced, distributed, or transmitted in any form or by any means, including photocopying, recording, or other electronic or mechanical methods, or by any information storage and retrieval system without the prior written permission of the publisher.

FROM:

TO:

Granny loves you
More than you know
She'll always love you
Wherever you go.

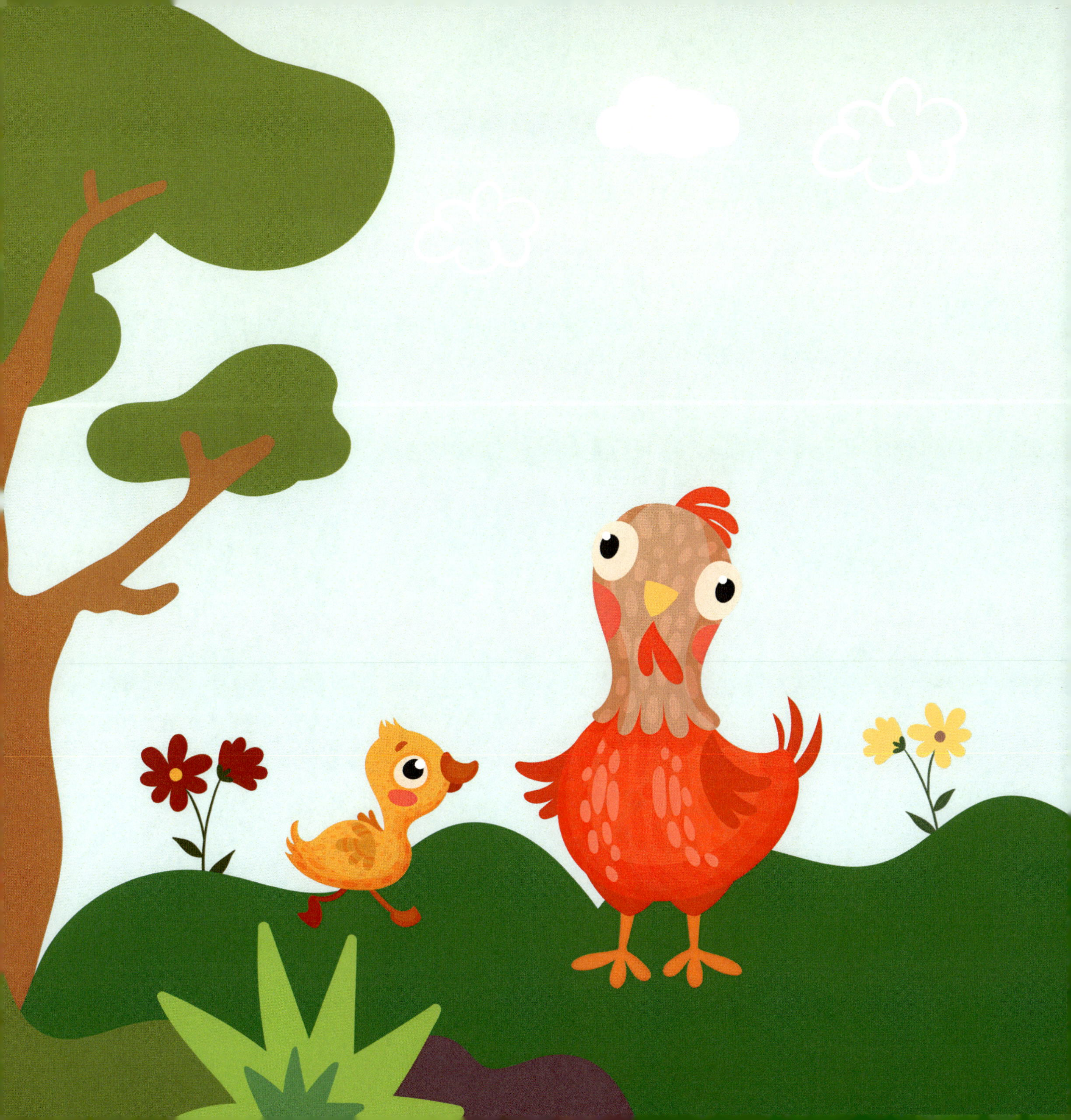

She'll hold you tight
With arms so warm
And keep you safe
From any harm.

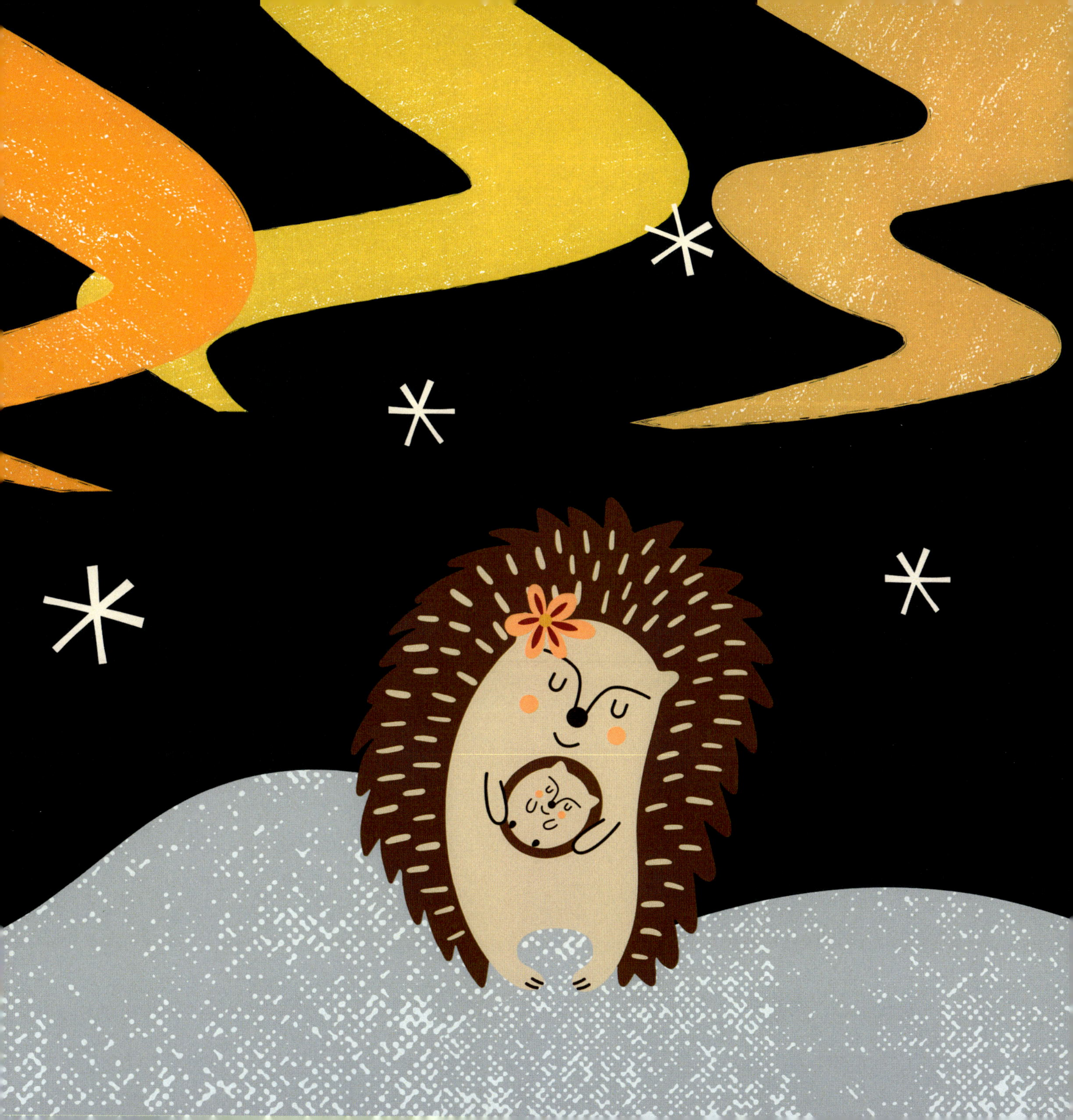

She'll always be proud
Of all you have made
And her love for you
Will never fade.

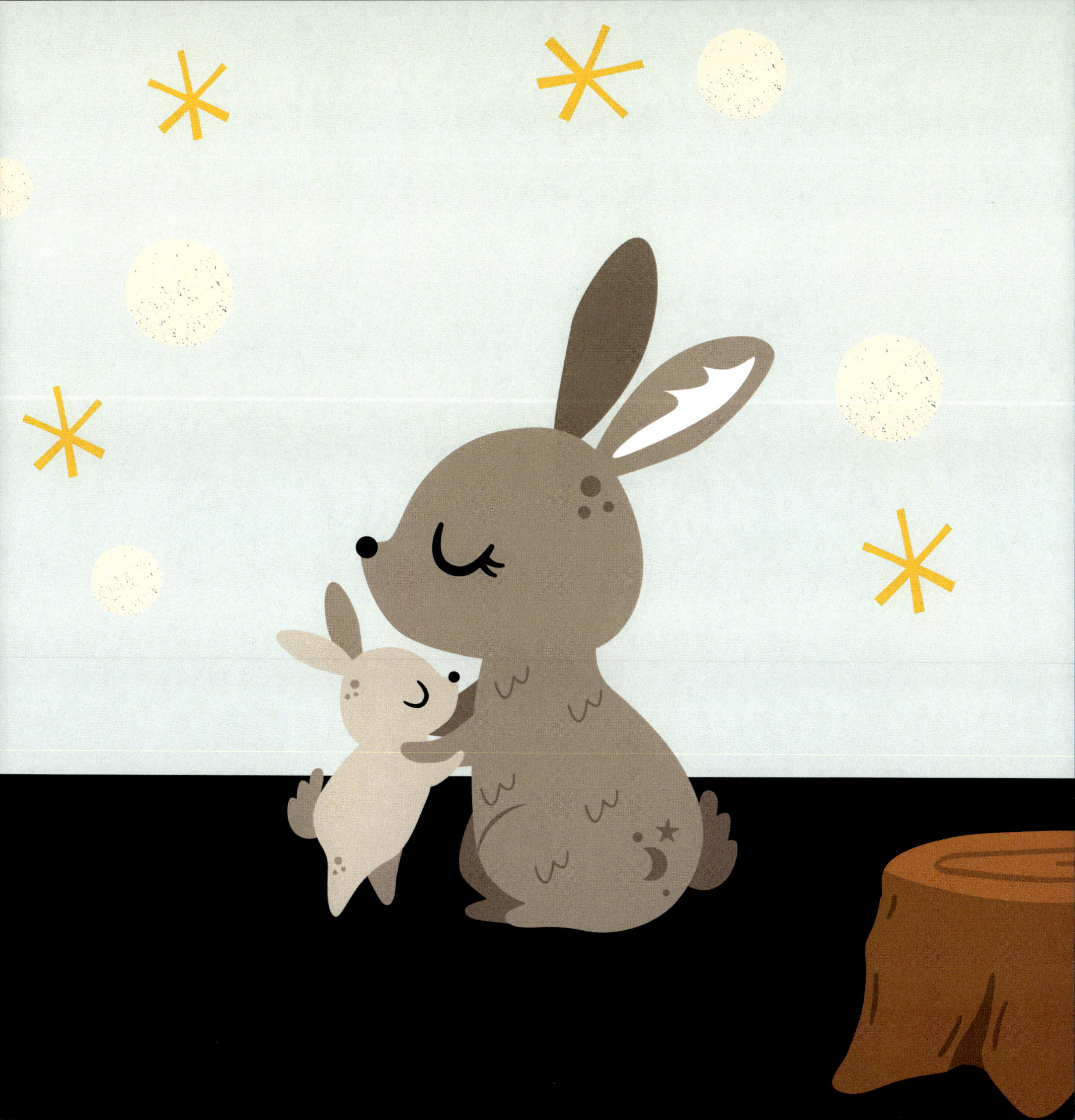

So always remember
Wherever you roam
Granny loves you
More than you know.

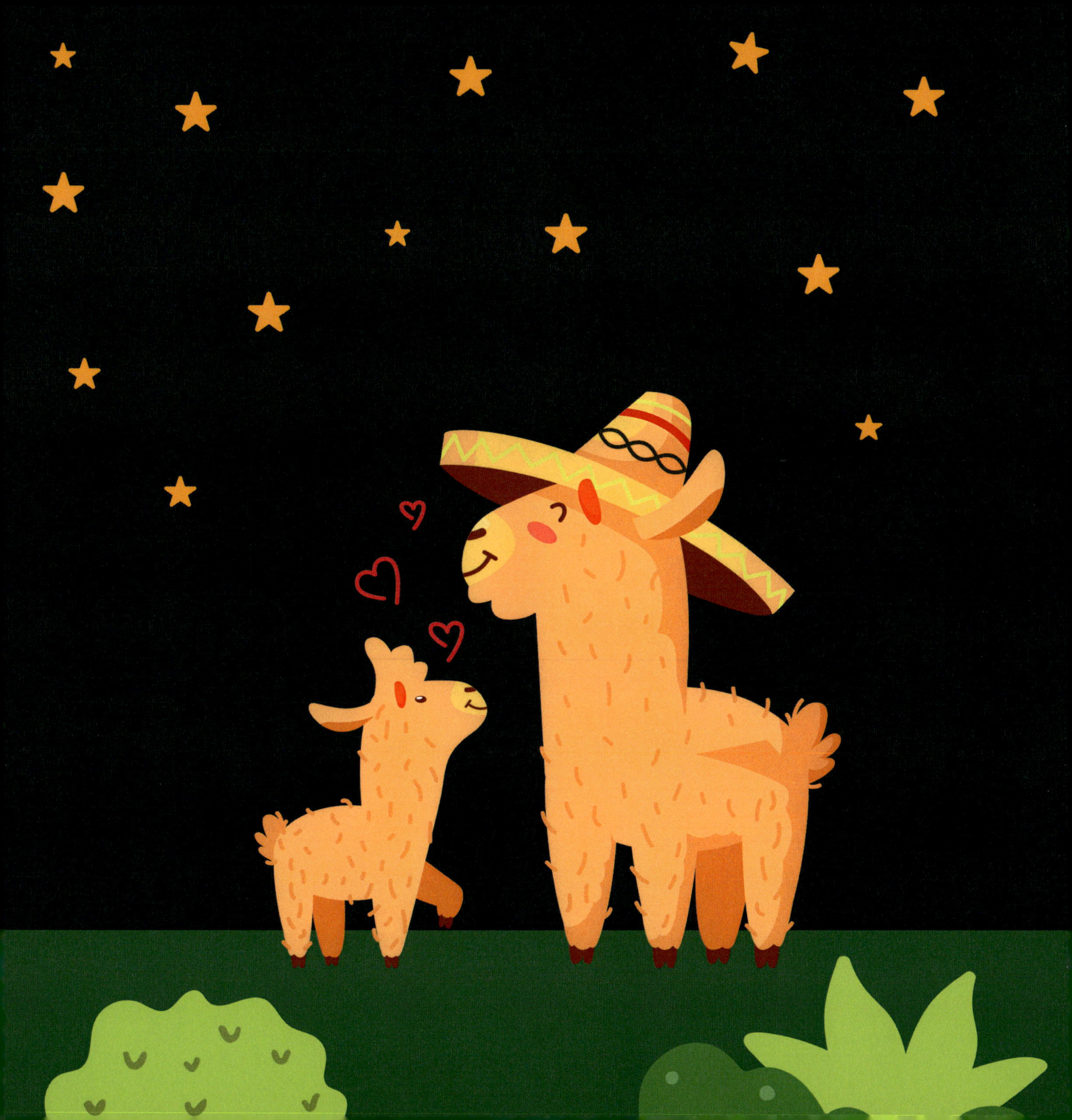

Her heart is full
Of love and care
She'll always be there
No matter where.

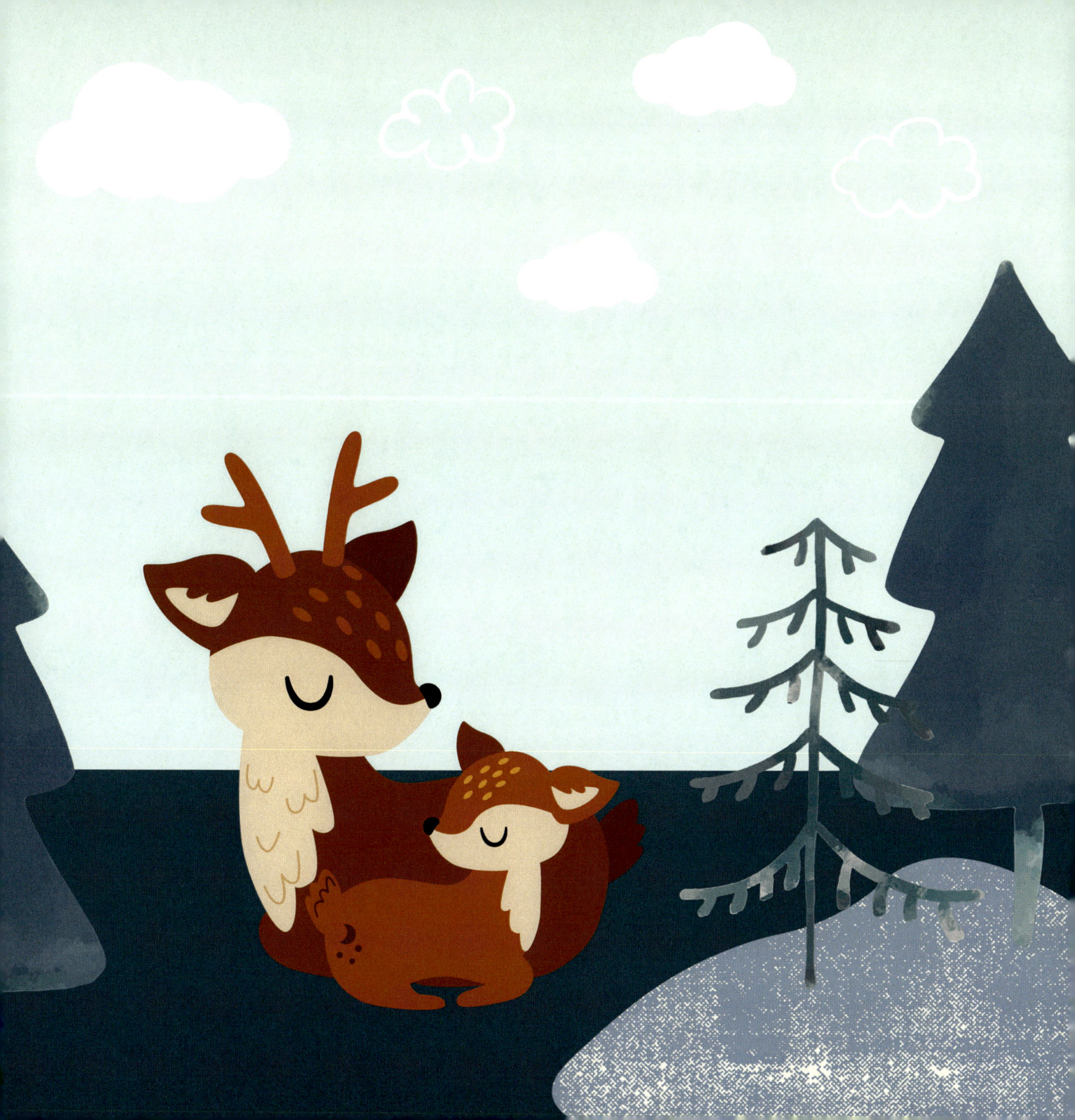

Her gentle heart
And giving hand
Will always be there
To help you stand.

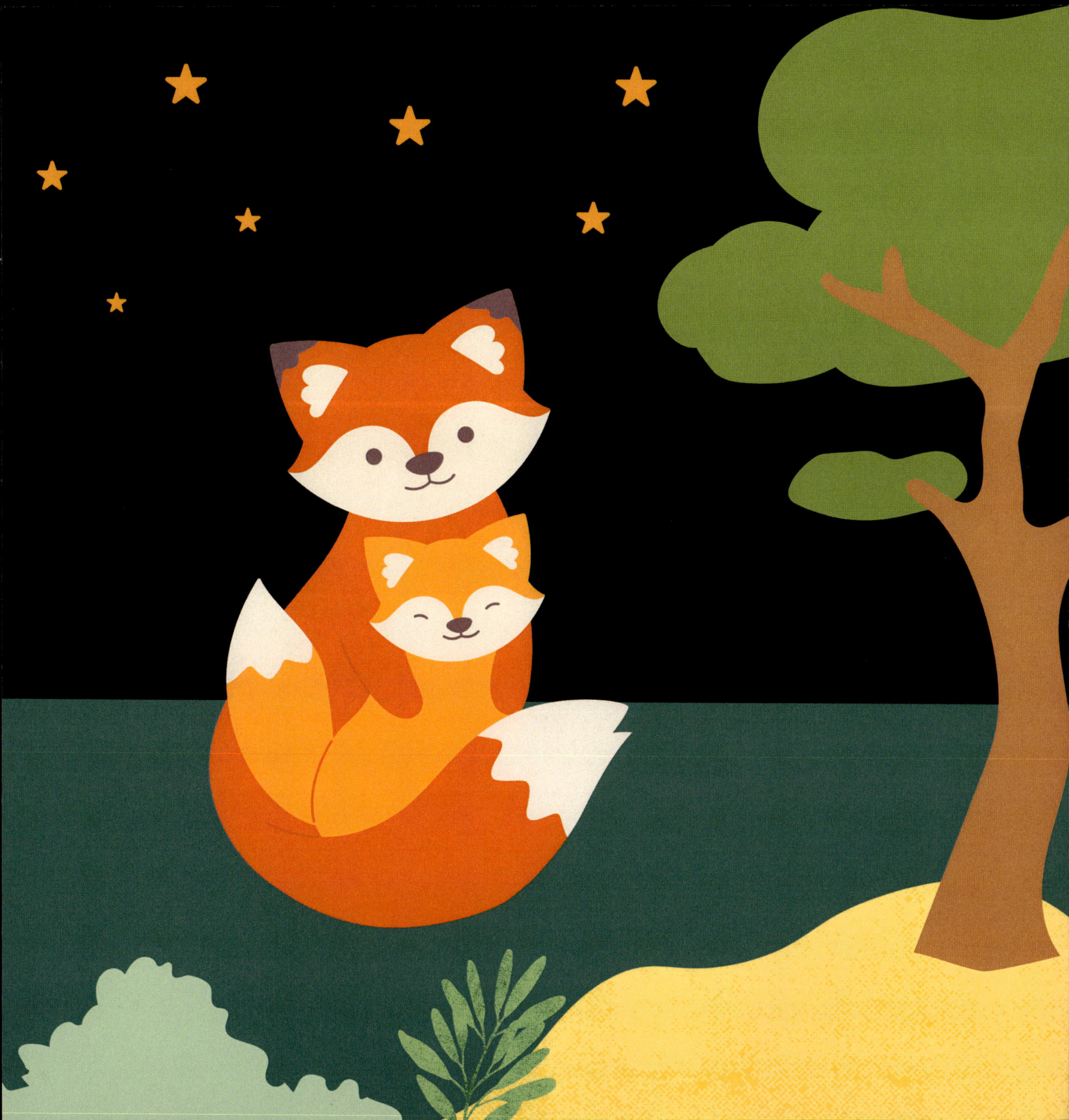

So know that no matter
Where you roam
Granny loves you
More than you know.

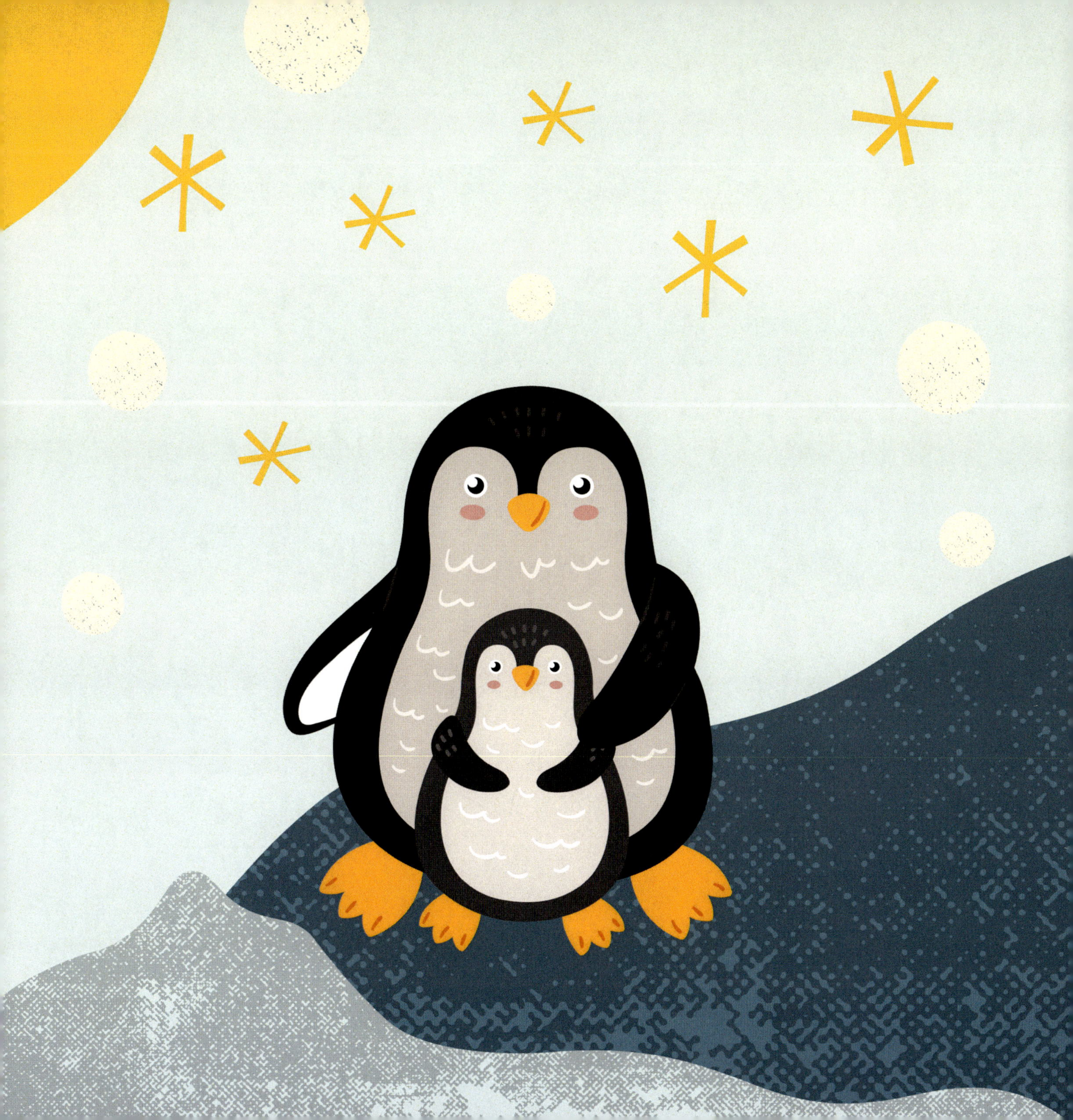

Her laughter will fill
You with **delight**
And her love will
Shine so **bright**.

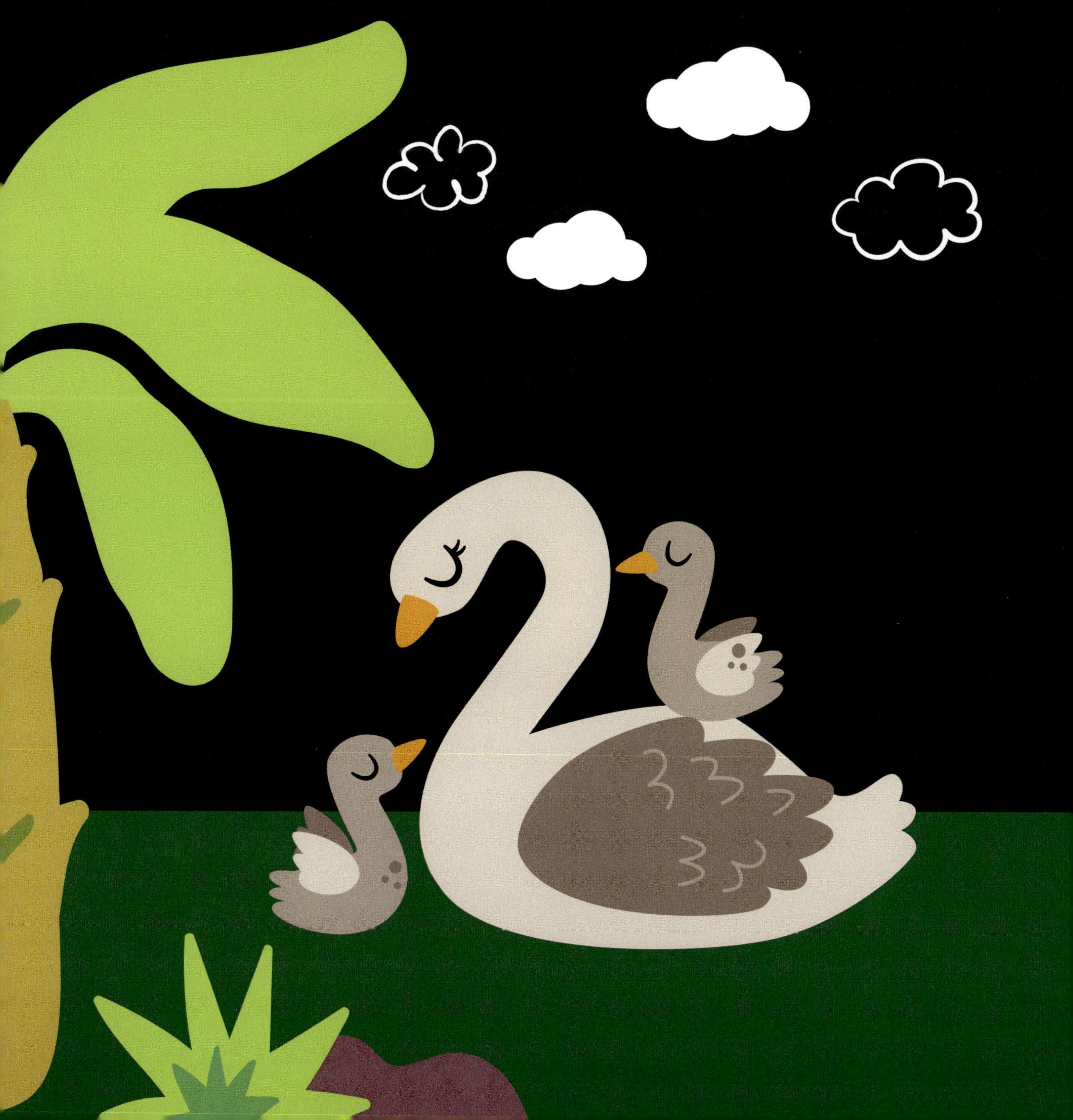

She'll listen to your
Laughter and tears
And wipe away
Your worries and fears.

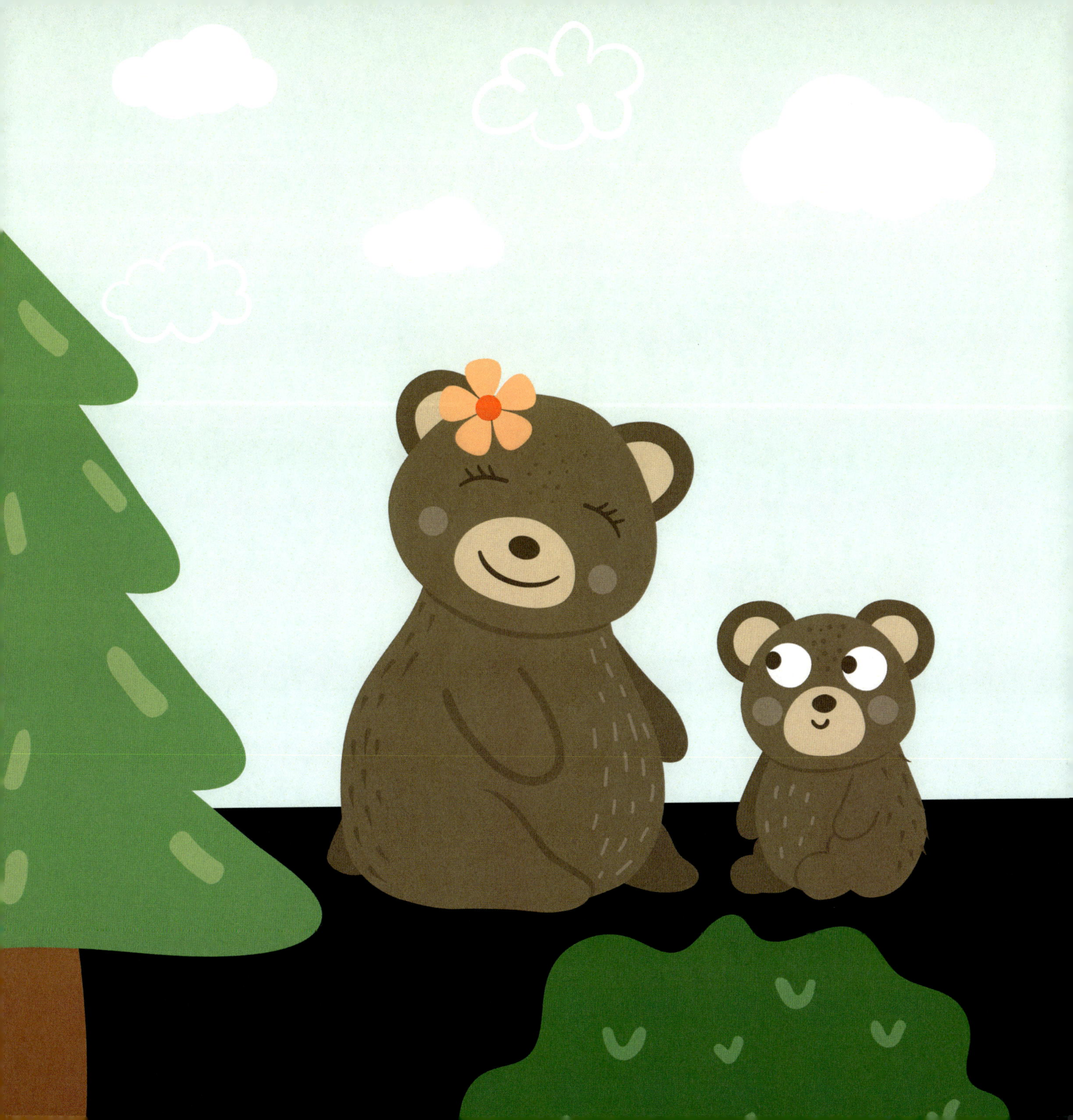

She'll be the one
Who believes in you
And helps you follow
Your dreams come true.

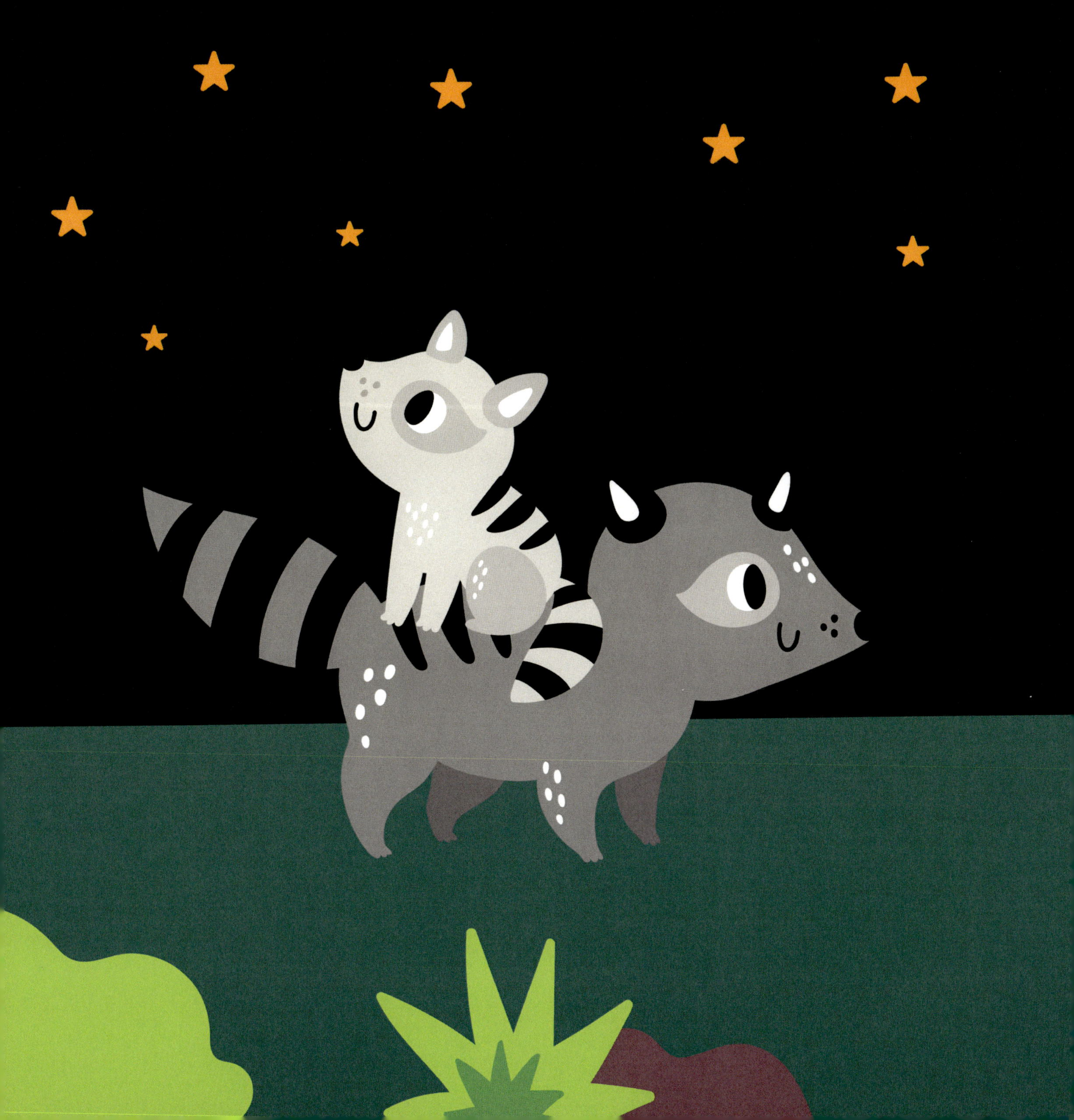

So always remember
Where you roam
Granny loves you
More than you know.

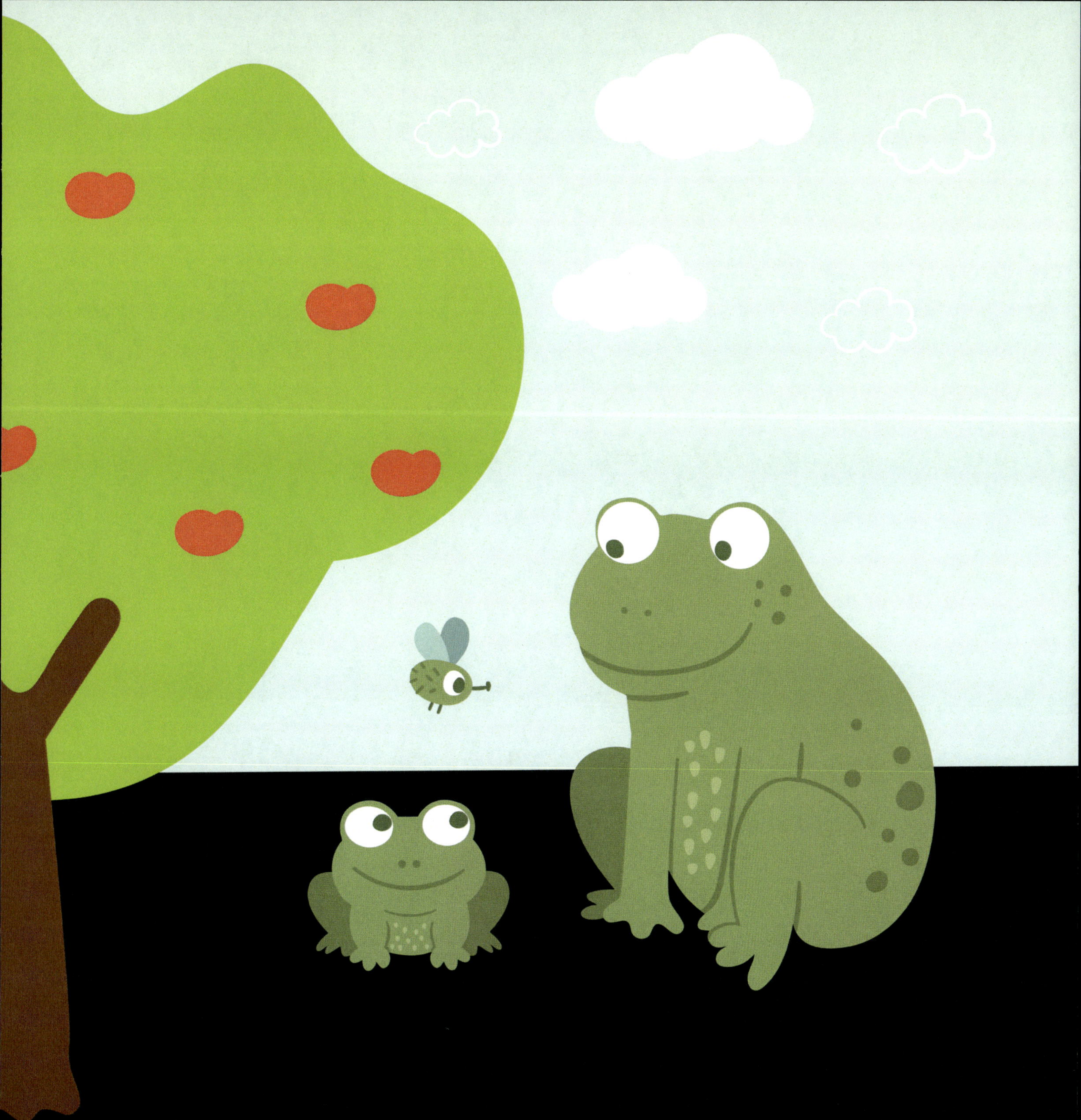

She'll hold your hand
And never let go
And always be there
To help you grow.

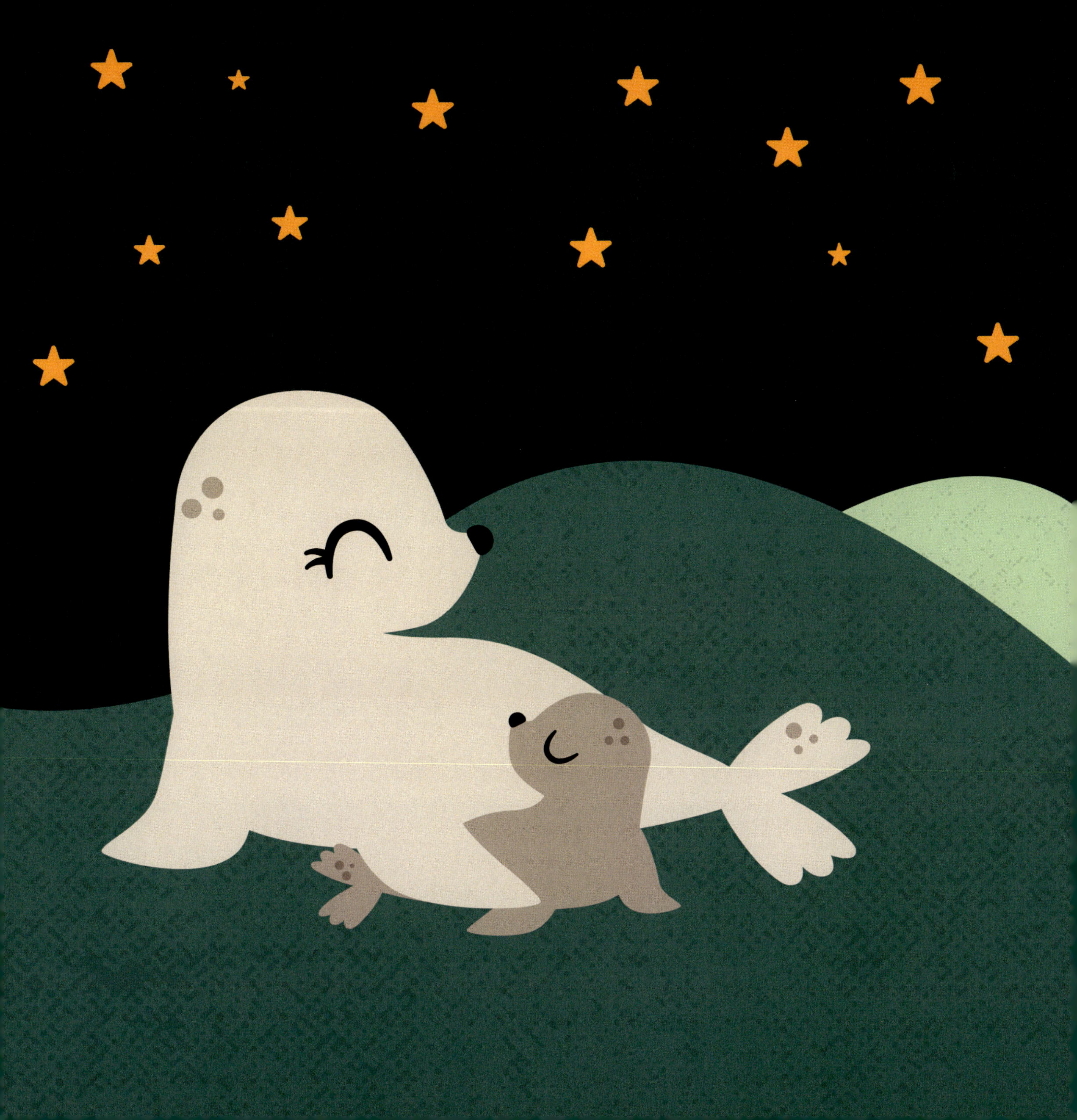

She'll teach you
The importance of giving
And show you
The beauty of living.

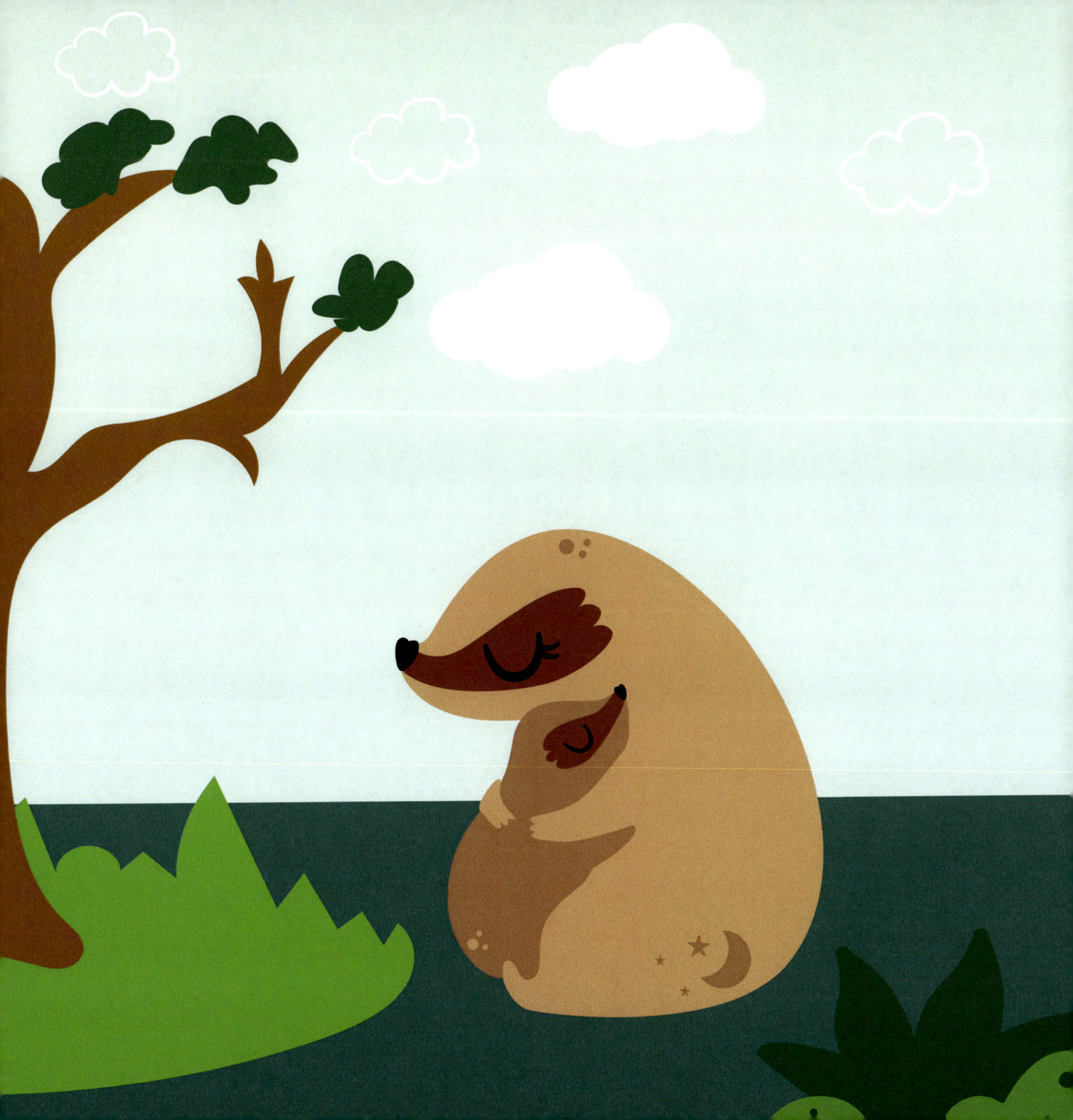

Her smile can

Light up any room

And her love for you

Will forever bloom.

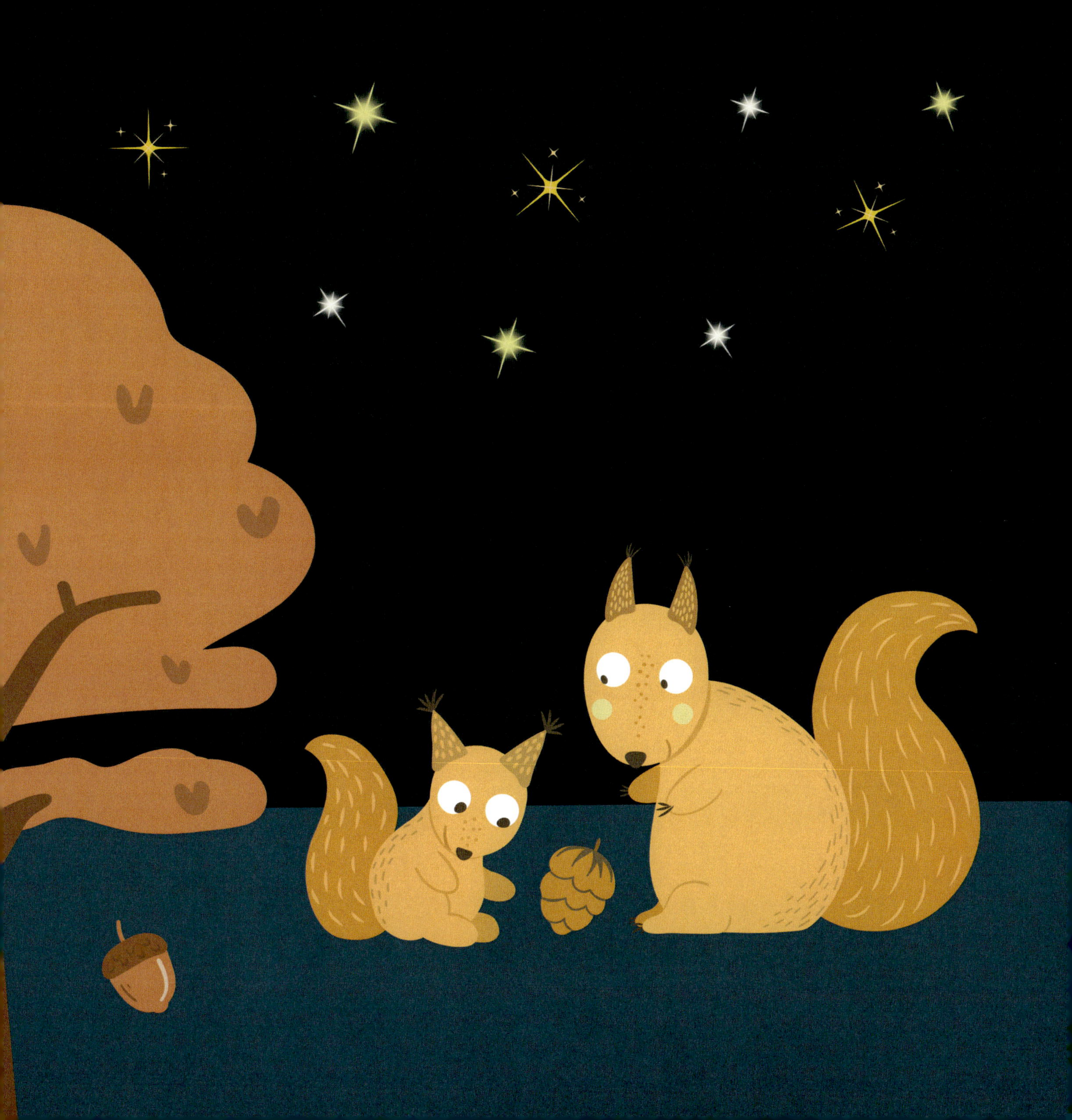

So never forget
No matter where you go
Granny loves you
More than you know.

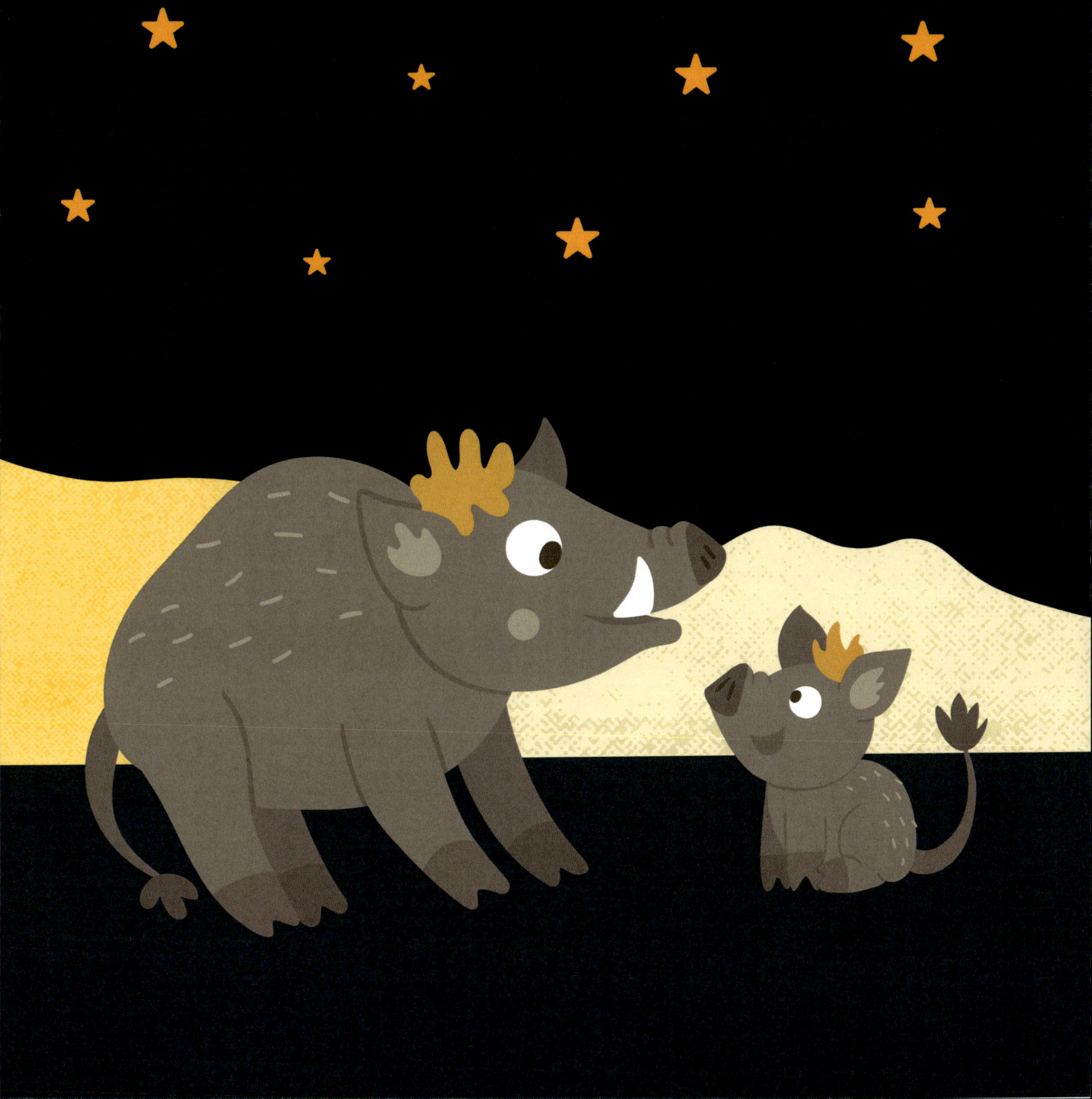

Did you know?

There are hidden bees throughout the book. Read the book again and see if you can find them all.

OTHER BOOKS IN THE 'LOVE YOU' SERIES

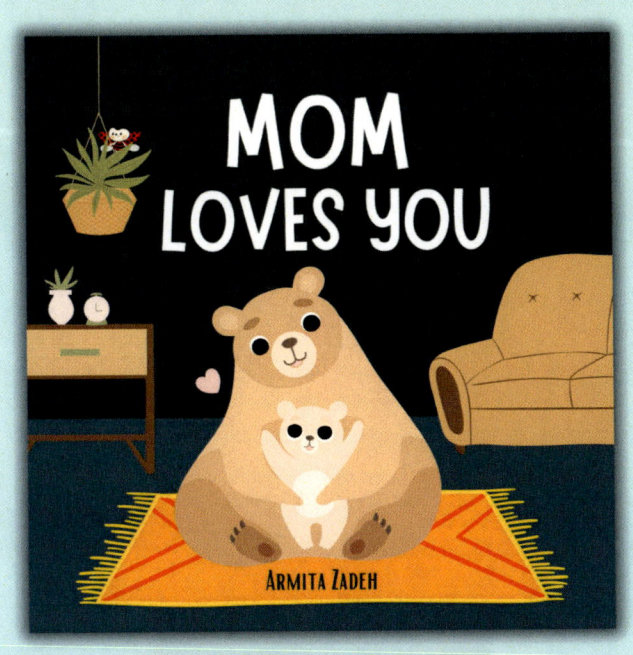

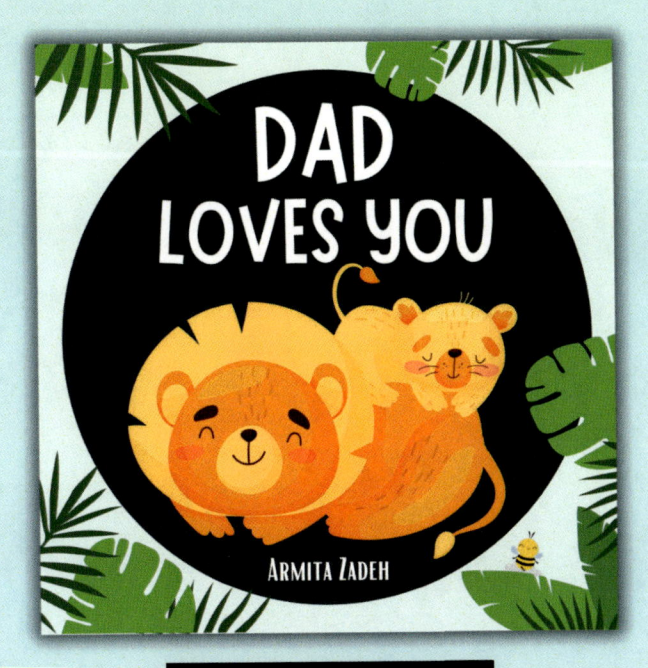

I would love to hear from you if you enjoyed this book. As a self-published author, I read every review and count every star. I'd be super grateful if you could leave an honest review on Amazon.

1

Made in United States
Orlando, FL
12 April 2025